How to Stop Stuttering and Stammering

A Guide to Getting Rid of a Stubborn Stutter in 7 Easy Steps Without Expensive Speech Therapy

by William Mauphrey

Table of Contents

Introduction 1

Chapter 1: Mentally and Physically Relax 7

Chapter 2: Talk to Yourself 13

Chapter 3: Break Eye Contact 19

Chapter 4: Use Breathing Exercises for Easier Speech 25

Chapter 5: Set a Rhythm to Your Speech 29

Chapter 6: Visualize the Words You Will Say 33

Chapter 7: Get Your Family and Friends Involved . 37

Conclusion 41

Introduction

Stuttering, also known as stammering, is an embarrassing condition in which we try to get a word out, but will often involuntarily repeat or prolong a sound, syllable, word or phrase. It occasionally happens to just about every human on earth. Sometimes, stuttering comes in the form of silence, when someone is unable to produce any sound. There are some people who live with the condition, and it is a real problem that affects their daily speech. It is thought that about 1% of the world's population stutters, and in the US alone, that's the equivalent to an amount somewhere in between the population of Chicago and the population of Los Angeles. Men account for about eighty percent of this number.

Can you imagine that you are giving a speech on an important issue, when you begin stuttering on not one, but many of the words in your speech? In this situation, your audience will most likely either find it somewhat amusing, or they'll pity you. Nobody wants to be laughed at, let alone pitied. The fear of receiving either one of these reactions sometimes causes the stammer to get even worse. However, experts say that we should not see this as the sole cause of a stammer. In these situations, nervousness about stuttering does cause it to worsen. But while this may be partially true, the cause of stutters is not really psychological.

Experts tend to believe that the primary cause of stuttering is either physiological or genetic.

Symptoms of stuttering will often appear in childhood when learning language skills. So what really are the mechanisms behind stuttering? It's still a mystery to scientists. What they do know for sure is that the causes of a person's stuttering can be developmental, neurogenic or psychogenic. One would think that psychogenic stuttering is the most common of them all, but it is actually the rarest. Neurogenic stuttering is caused by brain traumas such as stroke or head injury. Developmental stuttering occurs when children are learning how to talk, and the stutter that they have is not outgrown. This is the most common type.

Luckily, if you have this problem, you don't have to live with it for the rest of your life. There are many ways to get over your stutter without the expense of a speech therapist. In this book, we're going to take a look at seven of these ways, and how you can benefit from them daily to get rid of this frustrating and embarrassing condition.

© Copyright 2014 by LCPublifish LLC - All rights reserved.

This document is geared towards providing reliable information in regards to the topic and issue covered. The publication is sold with the idea that the publisher is not required to render accounting, officially permitted, or otherwise, qualified services. If advice is necessary, legal or professional, a practiced individual in the profession should be ordered.

- From a Declaration of Principles which was accepted and approved equally by a Committee of the American Bar Association and a Committee of Publishers and Associations.

In no way is it legal to reproduce, duplicate, or transmit any part of this document in either electronic means or in printed format. Recording of this publication is strictly prohibited and any storage of this document is not allowed unless with written permission from the publisher. All rights reserved.

The information provided herein is stated to be truthful and consistent, in that any liability, in terms of inattention or otherwise, by any usage or abuse of any policies, processes, or directions contained within is solely and completely the responsibility of the recipient reader. Under no circumstances will any legal responsibility or blame be held against the publisher for any reparation, damages, or monetary loss due to the information herein, either directly or indirectly.

Respective authors own all copyrights not held by the publisher.

The information herein is offered for informational purposes solely, and is universal as so. The presentation of the information is without contract or any type of guarantee assurance.

The trademarks that are used are without any consent, and the publication of the trademark is without permission or backing by the trademark owner. All trademarks and brands within this book are for clarifying purposes only and are the owned by the owners themselves, not affiliated with this document.

Chapter 1: Mentally and Physically Relax

A scenario in which the most fluent of speakers tend to stutter and stammer is a romantic encounter. Most of us have been in this situation before, where we see one of the most beautiful people we've ever seen and, when we finally muster the courage to talk to them, we utter something unintelligible. A simple trick to get over these nerves is to mentally relax. When we are nervous, our brains fire off information at a much more rapid pace and the body prepares itself for "fight or flight." This is why, in these situations, our hearts race and we get jittery. In this fast-moving, jumbled mess, the information our brain fires off that is needed for thinking and speech is also jumbled, and we struggle to know what to say or do next.

Most, if not all, of this jumbling occurs in the mind of the stutterer. When minds are always racing, even if hearts are not, a person ends up trying to say a bunch of things at once, when they really only want to say one thing at a time. Therefore, one of the most effective ways in dealing with a stutter is to relax; calm your mind and your body so you can focus better mentally. There are many ways that you can force your body to relax. We've outlined some here:

1. **Breathe**

    Do breathing exercises. Take breaks throughout the day and focus on your breathing technique. To do this, just sit up tall and straight, close your eyes and place your hand on your stomach. Next, inhale slowly through the nose, focus on how the air is working its way into your abdomen, and exhale through your mouth. Even though psychological causes for stammering like stress are rare, it is still good to try to get rid of them and steady your heart rate.

2. **Meditation**

    Meditation is not only for proponents and adherents of Far East religions. There are a lot of studies that have proven the benefits of meditation. Scientists have found that meditation alters your brain's neural pathways. This is great, as most stutters happen because of neural misfiring along these pathways. How to meditate? Just sit up straight, with both feet on the floor, then close your eyes and keep your focus on repeating something positive – a mantra. It doesn't have to be "Om," as you see a lot in movies. The mantra should add to the meditation process, so whisper something like "I am at peace with myself," or "I like feeling calm," or anything similar that you can say over and over again. Remember those breathing exercises? You will also need to sync your breathing with your mantra. Once you have done it right, you will be free of any or all distractions.

3. Friends and Family

One of the surest ways to relax your mind and body is through a social life: fun bonding times with the ones you love. Research has shown that your neurological pathways and circulation start to sync perfectly when you are in social bonding situations. So encourage these types of situations more often.

4. Understand Yourself

Get to know what puts your mind and body on edge, and what relaxes it. To do so, lie on your back, on your bed or on a mat on the floor, with your feet on the surface. Use your hands to observe how your body feels from your toes straight up to your scalp. Move from one part of your body to the next, feeling how your breath flows to that body part with each set of slow breaths. Ensure you don't go too fast.

5. Laugh

The best way to relax your mind and body – which you probably don't do enough – is to laugh. More and more research is supporting the old adage that laughter is the best medicine. Laughter lowers the body's stress hormone, cortisol, and boosts the mood-enhancing brain chemicals called endorphins. Once in a while, turn on the television or go on Netflix and find your favorite comedy or show, and let yourself have a good gut-busting laugh here and there. Let the neighbors complain.

6. Exercise

Some of you may be tired of seeing the same old thing almost every day: articles stating the many benefits of exercise. But it is true that exercise does your body and mind good in so many ways. Exercises such as walking, running, or even yoga, will cause the production of mood-enhancing chemicals in the brain, and produce other chemicals that can help you effectively deal with stress.

There are other ways to put your mind and body at ease but, while these things may work for some, they may not work for all. You just have to be familiar with your body and how it works. Only you can determine what really is best for you.

Chapter 2: Talk to Yourself

The mirror is not only for checking out your good looks. For the stutterer, it is an important tool to help get rid of this annoying condition. As was said earlier, having one-on-one conversations is hard for the stutterer, as they often try to say one thing but, in their mind, they are trying to say a whole lot of things at once. One of the best ways to beat this thing is to stand in front of the mirror and master the art of conversation. Actually, you will need to try mastering the art of speaking in general, since stuttering on stage at a public event is one of the most embarrassing things that could happen. There are different techniques that public speakers and conversationalists use, and we will teach them to you here.

The amount of time needed to practice depends on your daily schedule, but that should be your primary objective: fitting it into your daily schedule. Try to do this for at least a half hour per day. Talking to yourself is not the same as talking to another person, of course, but this exercise will help improve muscle memory of speech, which will boost your confidence. And with your confidence boosted, you will be more inclined to speak up in other environments when you have something to say, and you'll certainly be able to make new friends more easily. These types of advances will, in turn, give you more confidence, which will again, make you more likely to speak up.

It's a cyclical propulsion forward that starts simply from talking to yourself in the mirror.

The first step in fixing your speech impediment with a mirror is to speak clearly. Don't worry about your stutter right now. A chronic stutterer will be afraid to speak clearly, and will often speak under their breath. Start by reciting a passage from Shakespeare, or any other favorite, and use hand gestures. Enunciate your words and choose a volume that is clearly audible but, at the same time, won't disturb anyone around you. You have to master speaking clearly and use simple words at first to get your point across, then you can move up in the English language. As a matter of fact, take a break right now from reading this, stand or sit in front of a mirror and, for two minutes, speak about a single topic – tennis shoes, for instance – with the simplest of words you can find. Remember the tips that we mentioned above.

The next step we'll discuss that you should do in front of the mirror is improving your flow. Fluency is good, as it helps people to understand you without having to concentrate on what you're saying too much. Just think of a German with limited English-speaking proficiency giving a public speech. It is harder to follow what he is saying than a fluent English speaker, because you have to concentrate on what he is saying, or what he is trying to say. So flow is very important. The best way to improve your fluidity is to slow down! That's right, as a stutterer, you are likely trying to speak way too quickly. So in the mirror, even if you start to bore yourself to sleep, start speaking very slowly. If there are awkward pauses in your own speech, try adding a filler word, for example "um." Believe it or not, this is something that most people do subconsciously, so you won't stand out from the crowd with these filler words. However, as you know, filler words aren't a good habit either, so only use them as a stepping stone, knowing that later you'll have to quit the habit of filler words too. But for now, using these words will help you pause for a moment, think of the direction your conversation is going and get back on track.

Your next mirror exercise is to choose a topic of interest, and then give a 5 minute speech about it into the mirror. This is where you will truly be tested, as it is easy to stop speaking clearly and break word flow when you are, for instance, a gamer talking to yourself about the new upcoming Halo game. If you don't have many topics that excite you enough to speak on them for five minutes, then find something! Search the internet, read a magazine, look in the newspaper – whatever it takes. As you're performing your 5 minute speech, try to notice and count the number of times you stutter, just by using a pencil and scratch pad and adding a quick mark each time so as not to distract from your speech. When you're done, start all over again. It doesn't matter if the actual content of the speech is the same or not.... You can even make it up as you go. The second time around, again, count the number of times you stutter. Slowly, and over time, you'll notice that the number goes down.

If you're still wondering what topic to choose, and what you could possibly say about it for 5 whole minutes, rest assured, that part really doesn't matter and you should just find a way to blabber on about something. I'll give you a quick example, choosing the topic of "cucumbers." (Pretty random, right?):

> *"Cucumbers are green. Actually they are very light green on the inside, and yet the thick protective skin is a much darker color green. Cucumbers are healthy to eat, and they go with a lot of different foods. You can add them to salads, eat them whole as a snack, or even slice cucumbers and put them on your sandwich. That adds a nice crunch to any good sandwich. I've never heard of anyone cooking a cucumber, although I don't see why you couldn't do that too. Maybe it doesn't taste good that way. Gardening cucumbers can be a fun and relaxing activity. If you choose to do that, you'll need a piece of land, and very rich soil. If you don't like gardening, then it's best to get your cucumbers from the grocery store or farmer's market......"*

See how easy that was? I just picked a random topic, then started speaking about it completely impromptu, as if I was a cucumber expert standing on stage at a large vegetable conference. The exercise becomes even easier if you choose a topic you're actually into.

Once you've practiced these five minute speeches for a while, and you've noticed the number of times you stutter has dropped quite a bit, then next you may consider making your speaking style even better by paying attention to subtle nuances such as your volume, intonation, story-telling skills, pace, rhythm, and humor. Great conversationalists and public speakers are masters of these elements. Of course none of these are required to rid yourself of a stubborn stutter, but they will help you feel more confident when speaking, and it's the confidence that ultimately reduces the stuttering.

Chapter 3: Break Eye Contact

When you're practicing your conversations in the mirror, of course you will want keep eye contact. However, if you have not yet mastered speaking to yourself in the mirror, then in situations where you are speaking to someone, or speaking in public, you will have to break eye contact. You might ask, isn't that counterintuitive? Isn't the whole point of having a conversation to relate to a person on all levels, and to hold their attention with your eyes? Well, in some cases, you will need to break eye contact to keep from stuttering; but don't look up in the sky, or turn your back to your audience. The trick is to be able to speak to someone while looking like you are keeping eye contact. They will hardly notice the difference.

This step is easier for some than others. Some people find it especially hard to hold eye contact in any situation, and have learned how to break it without seeming rude or distant during conversations. One technique to use in these situations is to only look into the person's eyes periodically. Do this especially at the most important parts of the conversations, so they will know that you really are listening. For instance, if the person with whom you are dialoguing says that her cat died, that would be the time you look directly into her eyes, while offering your condolences. But what you say at that moment cannot be too lengthy, or you will risk stammering again. So keep your response to a minimum and look away. But where will you look?

One of the best places to look, from the perspective of someone who struggles to keep eye contact in everyday speech, is directly over the shoulder. When you are doing this, nine times out of ten, the person you are speaking to won't even notice. At different intervals, you will lock eye contact, but for no more than two seconds. The trick in not giving your technique away is to give other indicators that you are listening. There are many indicators, and you can use most of them in one conversation.

Let's discuss some of the indicators that you can use. One of these is to be quiet. Don't interrupt when the other person is talking. But you don't want to be too quiet, or the person will then wonder if you are really listening, or if your mind wandered off to "La La Land." The next tip is to encourage the person to continue speaking by nodding, or saying things like "mhmm", or "ok." Saying anything affirmative will give the impression you really are listening, and take the person's mind off the fact that you aren't looking into their eyes. Make sure that you give the right affirmations for the conversation, as saying things like "ok" when the person is expressing grief can be extremely rude. Make sure to continue summarizing what the person is saying, even if you don't agree with it. This gives the impression to the listener that you are interested in his/her point of view. During your summaries, you will want to make the occasional eye contact, but don't hold it for too long or you may get in trouble.

When it is your time to speak, you will want to avoid eye contact as much as possible, as stuttering will be even more prominent with prolonged eye contact. When speaking, keep your mind relaxed, while still focusing enough to understand what you are saying. This will ensure that you are speaking in the clearest language possible. Remember, like before, that you don't want to avoid eye contact for too long or you will make them uncomfortable. So, when you are speaking, stare into their eyes, if only for a second. This will be most effective at the high points of your conversation.

Of course, not all conversations will be held with just one individual. It can be really embarrassing to start stammering when speaking publicly, and it often gets worse because you are trying so hard to avoid people making fun of you. In show business, stage fright is something that effects even the most experienced of actors. One way to mitigate this is to shine bright lights directly on the performer. To the audience, it seems like the lights are just making them focus on the actor; but, to the actor, it makes the audience disappear. Those lights are very bright and don't allow the eyes to focus on the dark areas beyond, where the audience sits. This allows the performer to act like there is no one out there. They do this with speeches as well, although it doesn't happen all the time. So what should a person do if there are no lights to prevent them from seeing the audience? Well, one of the best things you can do is to have those stage lights in your own mind, preventing yourself from seeing the audience by pretending they aren't there. In terms of eye contact, you can use the same techniques you use in one-on-one situations by looking down an aisle or at a door directly in front of you, or just behind the last row of audience members. This will make it appear that you are holding eye contact with your audience, when you really aren't. While speaking, you should be focused somewhat on what you are saying, but in the proper way, so as not to fumble over your words.

Chapter 4: Use Breathing Exercises for Easier Speech

We briefly described breathing exercises earlier, but they cannot be overstated. Stutterers usually have trouble breathing while they are stuttering. Remember the "fight or flight" response? Stutterers will often go into "adrenaline mode" as they try their best to get their points across, and often forget to take a breath. To get your words flowing again and improve your speech, breathing exercises can help drastically.

Breathing exercises are not only for your home. They can be done right before you start talking to someone. Before you start to speak, take a couple of deep breaths. This will clear your airways and relax your nerves and mind. The breaths you take need to be held for a few seconds for it to work effectively. When you do this, you will feel how stressed you are because it will be easier to hear and feel your heart beating when you are holding your breath. However, if you are already in a social conversation, then it would be too late to do this, as it would make you look quite awkward if you did. What you should do is breathe deeply and slowly through your nose, especially when the other person is talking, to prepare yourself for the next time you need to say something.

When you stutter during conversations, you will often forget to breathe. So it is important to give yourself time to take a breath. Don't try to ramble for five minutes; instead, break your speech down into individual minutes, or shorter periods if need be, and breathe in those intervals. It is also important not to speak too fast. This can't be said often enough, as one of the top reasons someone stammers is that they are speaking faster than their brain can process what they are trying to say. Everyone has a limit to how fast their brain can process language, so it doesn't make sense to try to become an auctioneer.

The way you do your breathing exercises is important. There are different ways for different occasions that will help you relax your mind and your body. One of the best breathing exercises is to consciously think about how long your inhale is, compared to your exhale. Try to make them the same length. Practice this exercise at home alone, and also right before you enter into a conversation with someone else. Even during the conversation, you can do it while you are listening and the other person is speaking, although be sure to still concentrate on what they're saying of course.

Next, try to practice abdominal breathing, which you can do alone at home. Abdominal breathing is where you have one hand on your chest and one on your belly, and you take a deep breath through the nose.

Your hands are on your chest and belly to make sure your torso fills up with enough air. You should do this for about 10 minutes per day.

Chapter 5: Set a Rhythm to Your Speech

Do you sing? Whether you sing as an amateur or professionally, on stage or in the shower, you will realize something that you may not have before: you don't stutter when you sing. Why is that? If you know of anyone that stutters when they sing, that is one of the rarest things in the world – probably rarer than finding a diamond in your back yard. There are many reasons for this, and speech experts are actually using this phenomenon to understand the mechanisms of stuttering and how to more effectively cure it.

What experts know so far is that, when a person sings, the brain functions a bit differently than when they talk. When we sing, our vocal chords, lips and tongue operate differently than we are talking. When we sing, there is basically no pressure, unless you sing professionally, of course. When we sing, we forget ourselves for a moment and let ourselves go. The last reason is that, when we sing, we usually know the words of the song by heart.

The words that a person sings are usually recited from memory, and the voice used is often smooth and easily delivered. So can we use these same singing techniques to treat our speech impediment? You may be delighted to know that yes, we can. As an exercise, try reciting Martin Luther King's "I Have a Dream" speech the same way he did. Do you recognize his method? When he gets to certain words, he prolongs them, like a preacher giving a sermon. You don't have to join a convent, but you can use the same techniques that preachers use: speak slowly, prolong your words and emphasize certain words.

Remember earlier that we spoke about working on the style of speech? This is basically the same thing. Here, you will focus on volume, intonation, pace, rhythm, gestures, humor and story-telling. If there is a speaker that has the exact style that you want to emulate, then go on YouTube, or use whatever medium you can, to watch how they conduct their presentations. Ask yourself how they use each of the skills mentioned above, and see which one of them you can take for yourself. Once you've identified your style, work on it every day. Go back to your mirror and practice your newfound speaking style there for at least 10 minutes every day.

Chapter 6: Visualize the Words You Will Say

Visualizing what you say is one of the most powerful methods in stutter reduction, but it is also one of the hardest. One of the ways that we try to get rid of our stammer is by easing the stress on our brain, but visualizing your words will take some amount of brain power. It takes a while to master this but, when it is done right, it actually helps a lot. When you imagine the words in your mind, you have basically claimed them and your brain will utter the exact phrase that is pictured. This method is almost foolproof if done properly. For it to work, you will need a clear picture of what you want to say.

Say, for instance, that you are telling your girlfriend a story about how when you were young, you used to play with your neighbor's pet dog named Daffodil. Words like "dog" and "Daffodil" may be hard for you to say without stuttering, so before you get to them, try to visualize the actual creature in your mind, and claim it as your own. When you see an image in your mind, somehow the word becomes much easier to say.

Another trick you may want to employ is, if you notice yourself repeatedly stuttering or having trouble with the same word, then make a note of it, and next time you're at the computer, go to thesaurus.com and find a replacement synonym. A synonym is a word that means the same thing as another word. For example, if you are stumbling over the word "jump," you could say "hop" instead. The trick is to use a synonym that is easier to clearly speak than the original word. This makes it roll off the tongue more easily.

There is another solution you can try that is effective, but very embarrassing. If you find yourself stumbling over a word, you could spell it out instead of trying to pronounce it. Spelling it out does not always need to be letter-by-letter, like "j-u-m-p," especially when trying to form longer words. You could also pronounce a word one syllable at a time. This might be embarrassing, but you will be satisfied knowing you got over the word.

Since visualizing uses up brain power, you will have to pause on occasion to properly visualize the word or phrase. Don't be afraid to do so, as silence is not always bad. Think of the silence as an opportunity to get your words formed correctly. Most people perceive silence as part of thoughtful speech, and you may therefore be perceived as being more intelligent for taking these pauses. Not such a bad unintended benefit, is it?

Chapter 7: Get Your Family and Friends Involved

The final task is to get the help of your family and friends. No one knows you more than the people to whom you are closest. If you have had a stammer for a very long time and converse often with your friends or family, you may not know it, but most times they don't even recognize the stutter, as they have grown accustomed to it. Since they understand and know you so well, you should use them as your reference points and coaches.

One way your family and friends can help you is by not responding to your statement until you are completely finished. Since they are so close to you, they may understand what you are trying to accomplish and want to save you some energy by helping you complete your statement. Let them know that you need to finish your sentences by yourself. Tell them you understand that they are trying to protect you, especially in public situations and when around strangers, but tell them that you need to be allowed to finish what you are saying. Of course, there are times when you will need help. Do not be afraid to look to a family member or friend and let them know that they should jump in and help you out. One of the good things about being close to someone is that you can often communicate solely with your eyes.

You can also ask them to help you by making sure you are using the techniques that you are learning here. Tell them to watch you and to make sure you are doing everything you can to avoid stuttering. Also, ensure that they don't get mad or angry at a third party who finds your stutter amusing. If you or your friend are in a situation like that, you should both keep the conversation going as if you don't realize the person finds the stutter amusing. After a while, the person will get the gist and start tuning out your stutter. Your friends and family are important for you to get your stutter under control, as well as for conquering any fears that may arise from it.

Conclusion

Many people go through their entire lives thinking that they are stuck with an embarrassing stutter when, most often, they don't have to be. It can be treated, and often very quickly if the right techniques are used. It all comes down to one thing, and that is your willingness to practice. You will often have to work on certain things on your own, sometimes daily.

If you're reading this because you have a child with a stutter or stammer, you should know that the best time to get rid of it is while they are still young. Stuttering may sound cute for a toddler, but parents should try to correct it as much as possible, and as soon as possible.

The steps outlined earlier can sometimes themselves seem burdensome, but it is important to take time with them, as stuttering is even worse. One should always remember to speak more slowly, to regulate their breathing, and to talk in simpler terms in order to speak more fluently. If you practice these three things, plus the others mentioned herein, your stutter will be gone before you know it.

Finally, I'd like to thank you for buying this book! If you found it helpful, I'd greatly appreciate it if you'd take a moment to leave a review on Amazon. Thank you!

Made in the USA
Middletown, DE
23 September 2019